Rasta Rules

144 Rastafarian Rules, Laws and Regulations

By
Empress

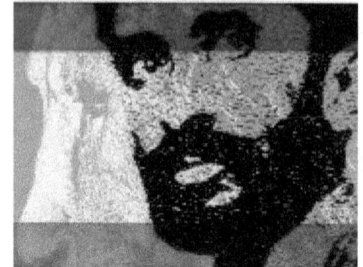

Rasta Way of Life

Life as a Rasta Woman

JAH RASTAFARI PRAYERS

Empress Yuajah

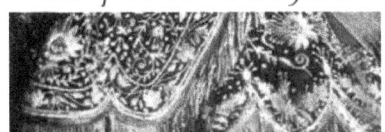

How to Become a King

EMPRESS

www.jamaicanrastafarianlove.com
www.jamaicanloveblog.wordpress.com

Give Thanks to King Selassie I and Empress Menen for their teachings, thanks to Jah for his mercies and forgiveness.
Thanks to the earth for being a source of life to all.
Blessed Love.

Table of Contents

5 Rasta Rules to think wisely	7
5 Rasta rules for using technology	10
13 Rasta Ital Food Laws	12
The Story of queen Esther (A Rasta Woman)	17
7 Rastafari Rules for Dreadlocks	32
The Story of Samson & Delilah	37
4 Rules for dressing as Queens	41
4 Bible scriptures on how Empress must dress	45
7 Rasta Rules for the home	47
5 quick Rasta rules/guidelines for marriage, and socializing	52
5 guidelines for Raising Rasta children	55
The Story of King Solomon's Wives	57
6 Rasta rules/guidelines for Ital Food cooking	59
20 Rasta Rules & Laws about sex	63
20 Various Laws for Rasta	66
6 Blessings of Obedience to Jah Rastafari	71
5 Punishments for breaking Jah Rastafari Rules	74
9 Rules of The Jah Rastafari Holy Sabbath	78
10 Rasta Rulesevery Rasta knows	81
3 Rasta Rules for Holiness and purity	82
5 King Selassie I Rules in Quotes	85

5 Important Rastafari Holidays 87

5 Rasta Rules to think wisely

#1 All experiences are really a "lesson in disguise" from Jah

Sometimes we go through things, we say "man why me" or, "God why is this happening? Rasta believe that in every experience, is a lesson from Jah, in disguise. This part of the book will not resonate with everyone only a select few.

Think deeper.

A story about looking Deeper: I once met a girl from overseas, she came here as a student to study in the home of 2 psychologists. She was no longer working there by the time we met, and had moved out. Every day she complained about her experience living with this "psychologist couple" and their 2 dogs, and their 2 kids.

One day after some deep meditation I explained to her the experience was not about all the small things she was complaining about at all, it was about living with 2 psychologists. How many people can say they have lived with 2 psychologists at the same time. No hands up? That is what I thought. I wanted to explain to her that there was a deeper lesson, just for her, from Jah. I said "Sarah, that experience you had, living with the two Psychologists...., it was not about the Psychologists, and how much they wronged you..." She understood what I was saying to her as, me siding with the Psychologists. She was not ready for the lesson. So just know as a Rasta, you have to know Jah himself is trying to show/tell you something in every experience, big or small.

I wanted to explain to her that she obviously had some issues to work on. One does not "just live with 2 psychologists" and don't learn a thing or 2, about how to handle yourself, your emotions, and your life.

#2 Jah is everywhere in everything
Jah is everywhere at all times. You can talk to him, ask him questions, etc. Jah is in nature abundantly. It is a good idea to have plants and small animals in the home, to bring more nature in as a Rastafari. Because Jah feels more welcome in these environments.

#3 Bible Study makes one wise
Bible study can bring more wisdom. It depends who you are already. Read the bible with openness and ask Jah to help you understand the bible in a spiritual sense. The bible is full of stories and sayings that need to be meditated on for understanding. Keep studying as a Tafari. Overstanding will come when the time is right.

#4 Think positive to get positive
Rasta believe we must see every experience in life *as a positive*. Every experience. Again we must try to see the lesson in disguise. Sometimes things happen we do not like but we must put a positive spin on it in our minds so that we stay connected to Jah at all times. **Negative thinking is separation from the creator.** Think positive at all times about all things.

#5 Children are a blessing from the creator

Rasta believe children are a blessing from Jah. We believe they are open and loving and can teach us about life in their simplistic way of looking at things. Rasta do not disrespect children. We talk to them with patience, love and respect for their perspective on life.

5 Rasta rules for using technology

#1 Technology to advance Rastafari?
A deep Rastafari will refuse to use technology, calling it "babylon" at its highest. But some do use Babylon technology to advance Rastafari such as myself. If you use your Technology to share Rastafari with the masses then it is deemed ok by most Rasta.

#2 Rasta do not look at porn
Rasta do not look at porn. We know pornography is a trick. Porn separates men and women from Jah, and makes them masturbate and become volatile.

#3 Rasta use technology responsibly
Rasta uses his technology responsibly. Facebook, cell phones, tablets, email, texting is not used by Rasta to hurt other people. This is against Rastafari livity and culture.

#4 Technology is not Rastafari identity

Rasta knows his technology is not who he is. That technology is just a tool on the journey. Rasta do not fall in love with technology. We know when we are home with family it is time for technology to be shut off and to live the way Jah intended. Jah did not create the earth with cell phone. This is man made.

#5 Rasta know when to turn off technology

Most people are addicted to some type of technology. Laptop cell phone, video games, xbox, tablet, facebook etc. Rasta know life is in Jah Rastafari not in technology. Rasta have a time to turn off the technology and allow those close to him to contact him the old fashioned way. That's just how it is. You can't have the technology (excluding music playing) running 24/7 like its a part of you, or like it is necessary for life….no!

13 Rasta Ital Food Laws

What is the meaning of "Ital food Diet" as a Rasta?

The word Ital in Rastafari means clean and natural. The words Ital food Diet, means food that is clean and natural, unpackaged and unprocessed, as much as possible.

13 Rasta Ital Food Laws

1. **Organic food** - Organic food that grows on a tree, out of the earth, on a bush etc. Not created by synthetic seeds etc. ..
2. **Unpackaged food** - Unpackaged food may be purchased at the bulk food store. Bulk oats for porridge, bulk granola for cereal etc. No canned food for Rasta. "Canned food" is one of the leading cancer causing foods.
3. **No meat no chicken or pork no shellfish** - No meat or pork for Rastafari (nothing that can be considered a caracas)
4. **No preservatives** - No Preservatives have a hard time breaking down in the body naturally. They are very unhealthy for the holy temple. (no canned food, no frozen food, no packaged food etc)
5. **Only natural sugars** - Only natural sugars for cooking Ital food, such as honey, molasses or cane sugar
6. **No salt added to foods** - No added salt for Ital food, or if one must, use natural salt added only (sea salt, Himalayan mountain salt)
7. **Most Rastas have stopped eating fish** - Fish used to be a very important part of the Ital food diet. But now with fish farming, Most Rasta have opted not to eat Fish.
8. **Natural cooking oil** - Only olive oil, or other natural oil such as coconut oil to cook food Rasta food.
9. **Most Rasta have stopped eating Eggs** - Most Rastafari have stopped eating eggs as food or eggs within our food.
10. **No alcohol** - No beer, no wine, no liquor for Rasta to drink. It is against the livity.
11. **Rasta eat white food in moderation** - White Potatoes, white rice, white pasta etc. is food to be eaten in moderation as it lacks nutritional value for the temple.
12. **Rasta eat refined sugar in moderation** - Rasta can eat a cookie or donut, but we know to do it *in moderation*.
13. **No cow's milk** - No cow's milk for Rasta to drink. Rasta drink almond, soya, or Rice Milk, We cook with coconut milk, or soya or almond milk as well.

As Tafari I find I buy most of my dry goods in bulk at the health food store, and I shop basically everyday for fresh organic greens etc to cook my dinner and food for the next day, each day. I do not believe in freezing and eating the next day, and I usually cook food that perishes pretty quickly. I keep, my chickpeas, lentils, yam food, and okra overnight sometimes for the next day if there is leftovers, but I usually have to go to the grocery store anyway for my daily salad. Give Thanks. (Try to buy organic only, GMO are very unhealthy)

Rasta enjoys a diet that adds nutrients to the body.

As a new Rasta you may eat these foods in small quantities, or not at all. The reason is *Rasta eats an ital food diet for spiritual reasons*. The more we adhere to the Rasta diet, the closer we draw to Jah. It's not for fun, or the enjoyment of personal restriction. It's to increase our Rasta spiritual meditations, and our [Jah Rastafari](#) spiritual awareness. Check out the [Rastafari meditation handbook to learn more.](#) When Rasta wants to substitute the white food he may eat…

- Brown rice instead of white rice
- brown whole grain pasta instead of white bleached pasta
- brown bread whole grain bread
- White Potatoes in moderation or orange potatoes
- White Yam in moderation, yellow yams

Deep Coloured foods have more nutrients

When it comes to food and health, black is beneficial. While green is hailed as the eco-health standard, new food research is revealing that the dark side of nature holds good things as well. According to doctors James Joseph and Daniel Nadeau (see Resources), "In the ORAC* tests at Tufts, blue foods quenched more free radicals than any other foods. Blueberries and blackberries were clear winners among fresh fruits; prunes and raisins among dried fruits." Indeed, dark-coloured fruits and vegetables are nutritional powerhouses...

Foods commonly eaten on a Rasta Ital food Diet....

- dark black beans
- wild rice
- Eggplant
- okra
- Lentils ([lentil soup recipe](#))
- beets
- broccoli
- Butternut Squash

- Pumpkin
- Broccoli
- Spinach
- Yam
- Rice
- Chocho
- Bop choy
- Onions
- Garlic thyme
- Oregano

Himalayan Salt Benefits

Rasta also may use Himalayan mountain salt, for food. When I did research on the benefits of Himalayan salt, the findings blew my mind. I conclude those of us not ingesting himalayan salt are missing out on a key part of health optimization.

Rasta use Himalayan Salt for food

Containing at least 84 naturally occurring trace elements in their natural mineral form...

The Story of queen Esther (A Rasta Woman)

The story of Esther begins with a grand banquet at the palace of King Ahasuerus, also referred to as King Xerxes. The king had become drunk on wine and commanded that his wife, Queen Vashti come out before everyone to show how beautiful she was. Queen Vashti refused to be paraded before everyone. King Xerxes was so angry at her disrespect and disregard for his request that he divorced her. The king called for a nationwide beauty pagent to be held to find a new beautiful queen.

A Jewish woman named Esther was taken with other young women to a citadel. Esther's cousin Mordecai had taken Esther in and raised her as his own after Esther's parents had died. A man named Hegai was put in charge of preparing the women for meeting the king. Esther's beauty won her Hegel's favor and she was given special attention. Esther was careful however to not tell anyone her nationality, as Mordecai had warned her not to.

When it was Esther's turn to go before the king, he immediately found her the most attractive and beautiful of all woman and placed the royal crown on her head. King Ahasuerus held a great banquet for his new queen, Esther. Esther continued to hide her Jewish background as Mordecai had instructed her to do because he knew it would be dangerous for her if anyone found out she was a Jew.

One night when Mordecai was sitting by the king's gate, he overheard two guards named Bigthan and Teresh conspiring to assassinate King Xerxes. Mordecai told Queen Esther of the plan and Esther told the king, giving credit to Mordecai for overhearing the plan. The two guards were hanged.

Mordecai then refused to bow down the Haman, the highest of all nobles. When Haman found out about this and that Mordecai was a Jew, Haman became enraged with anger and wanted to kill not only just Mordecai but all of the Jewish nation. Haman convinced King Xerxes to kill all Jews as they stood in opposition to the king's rule. King Ahasuerus agreed and set a date for all Jews to be killed.

Mordecai told Esther about the king's edict to kill all the Jewish people. Esther feared for her life and tried to avoid his request to do something. Mordecai again pleaded with Queen Esther to do something to save the people. Esther responded instructing all Jews to join her in fasting for three days and three nights, then she would approach the king with her request.

Esther went to King Xerxes after three days of fasting and the king asked her what her request was. Queen Esther asked that the king and Haman join her at a banquet the next day. The king said yes and asked Esther to let her request be known at the banquet. Haman was still so enraged with Mordecai that he went to set up a pole to impale Mordecai the morning before the banquet.

The king could not sleep that night and began to read the the book that contained all that had happened during his reign. The king read and was reminded of how Mordecai exposed the plot to assassinate the king. The king wanted to reward Mordecai for his good deed and he called Haman in to ask what should be done for a man who the king delights in. Human thought the king was talking about himself and responding saying extravagant gifts and honor. Haman was even more enraged when the king told him it was for Mordecai!

The next day was the banquet Queen Esther had called for. The king again asked Esther what her request was so he could grant her what she wanted. Esther boldly asked that she and her people be spared and that Haman had plotted to kill all Jews for money. The king was filled with anger against Haman and had him hanged on the very pole that Haman had set up for Mordecai.

Queen Esther and Mordecai were given Haman's estate. They were honored with royal garments and a decree was written to protect all Jews.

Esther 1

1 This is what happened during the time of Xerxes, the Xerxes who ruled over 127 provinces stretching from India to Cush : 2 At that time King Xerxes reigned from his royal throne in the citadel of Susa, 3 and in the third year of his reign he gave a banquet for all his nobles and officials. The military leaders of Persia and Media, the princes, and the nobles of the provinces were present. 4 For a full 180 days he displayed the vast wealth of his kingdom and the splendor and glory of his majesty. 5 When these days were over, the king gave a banquet, lasting seven days, in the enclosed garden of the king's palace, for all the people from the least to the greatest who were in the citadel of Susa. 6 The garden had hangings of white and blue linen, fastened with cords of white linen and purple material to silver rings on marble pillars. There were couches of gold and silver on a mosaic pavement of porphyry, marble, mother-of-pearl and other costly stones. 7 Wine was served in goblets of gold, each one different from the other, and the royal wine was abundant, in keeping with the king's liberality. 8 By the king's command each guest was allowed to drink with no restrictions, for the king instructed all the wine stewards to serve each man what he wished. 9 Queen Vashti also gave a banquet for the women in the royal palace of King Xerxes. 10 On the seventh day,

when King Xerxes was in high spirits from wine, he commanded the seven eunuchs who served him—Mehuman, Biztha, Harbona, Bigtha, Abagtha, Zethar and Karkas— 11 to bring before him Queen Vashti, wearing her royal crown, in order to display her beauty to the people and nobles, for she was lovely to look at. 12 But when the attendants delivered the king's command, Queen Vashti refused to come. Then the king became furious and burned with anger. 13 Since it was customary for the king to consult experts in matters of law and justice, he spoke with the wise men who understood the times 14 and were closest to the king—Karshena, Shethar, Admatha, Tarshish, Meres, Marsena and Memukan, the seven nobles of Persia and Media who had special access to the king and were highest in the kingdom. 15 "According to law, what must be done to Queen Vashti?" he asked. "She has not obeyed the command of King Xerxes that the eunuchs have taken to her." 16 Then Memukan replied in the presence of the king and the nobles, "Queen Vashti has done wrong, not only against the king but also against all the nobles and the peoples of all the provinces of King Xerxes. 17 For the queen's conduct will become known to all the women, and so they will despise their husbands and say, 'King Xerxes commanded Queen Vashti to be brought before him, but she would not come.' 18 This very day the Persian and Median women of the nobility who have heard about the queen's conduct will respond to all the king's nobles in the same way. There will be no end of disrespect and discord. 19 "Therefore, if it pleases the king, let him issue a royal decree and let it be written in the laws of Persia and Media, which cannot be repealed, that Vashti is never again to enter the presence of King Xerxes. Also let the king give her royal position to someone else who is better than she. 20 Then when the king's edict is proclaimed throughout all his vast realm, all the women will respect their husbands, from the least to the greatest." 21 The king and his nobles were pleased with this advice, so the king did as Memukan proposed. 22 He sent dispatches to all parts of the kingdom, to each province in its own script and to each people in their own language, proclaiming that every man should be ruler over his own household, using his native tongue.

Esther 2

1 Later when King Xerxes' fury had subsided, he remembered Vashti and what she had done and what he had decreed about her. 2 Then the king's personal attendants proposed, "Let a search be made for beautiful young virgins for the king. 3 Let the king appoint commissioners in every province of his realm to bring all these beautiful young women into the harem at the citadel of Susa. Let them be placed under the care of Hegai, the king's eunuch, who is in charge of the women; and let beauty treatments be given to them. 4 Then let the young woman who pleases the king be queen instead of Vashti." This advice appealed to the king, and he followed it. 5 Now there was in the citadel of Susa a Jew of the tribe of Benjamin, named Mordecai son of Jair, the son of Shimei, the son of Kish, 6 who had been carried into exile from Jerusalem by Nebuchadnezzar king of Babylon, among those taken captive with Jehoiachin king of Judah. 7 Mordecai had a cousin named Hadassah, whom he had brought up because she had neither father nor mother. This young woman, who was also known as Esther, had a lovely figure and was beautiful. Mordecai had taken her as his own daughter when her father and mother died. 8 When the king's order and edict had been proclaimed, many young women were brought to the citadel of Susa and put under the care of Hegai. Esther also was taken to the king's palace and entrusted to Hegai, who had charge of the harem. 9 She pleased him and won his favor. Immediately he provided her with her beauty treatments and special food. He assigned to her seven female attendants selected from the king's palace and moved her and her attendants into the best place in the harem. 10 Esther had not

revealed her nationality and family background, because Mordecai had forbidden her to do so. 11 Every day he walked back and forth near the courtyard of the harem to find out how Esther was and what was happening to her. 12 Before a young woman's turn came to go in to King Xerxes, she had to complete twelve months of beauty treatments prescribed for the women, six months with oil of myrrh and six with perfumes and cosmetics. 13 And this is how she would go to the king: Anything she wanted was given her to take with her from the harem to the king's palace. 14 In the evening she would go there and in the morning return to another part of the harem to the care of Shaashgaz, the king's eunuch who was in charge of the concubines. She would not return to the king unless he was pleased with her and summoned her by name. 15 When the turn came for Esther (the young woman Mordecai had adopted, the daughter of his uncle Abigail) to go to the king, she asked for nothing other than what Hegai, the king's eunuch who was in charge of the harem, suggested. And Esther won the favor of everyone who saw her. 16 She was taken to King Xerxes in the royal residence in the tenth month, the month of Tebeth, in the seventh year of his reign. 17 Now the king was attracted to Esther more than to any of the other women, and she won his favor and approval more than any of the other virgins. So he set a royal crown on her head and made her queen instead of Vashti. 18 And the king gave a great banquet, Esther's banquet, for all his nobles and officials. He proclaimed a holiday throughout the provinces and distributed gifts with royal liberality. 19 When the virgins were assembled a second time, Mordecai was sitting at the king's gate. 20 But Esther had kept secret her family background and nationality just as Mordecai had told her to do, for she continued to follow Mordecai's instructions as she had done when he was bringing her up. 21 During the time Mordecai was sitting at the king's gate, Bigthan and Teresh, two of the king's officers who guarded the doorway, became angry and conspired to assassinate King Xerxes. 22 But Mordecai found out about the plot and told Queen Esther, who in turn reported it to the king, giving credit to Mordecai. 23 And when the report was investigated and found to be true, the two officials were impaled on poles. All this was recorded in the book of the annals in the presence of the king.

Esther 3

1 After these events, King Xerxes honored Haman son of Hammedatha, the Agagite, elevating him and giving him a seat of honor higher than that of all the other nobles. 2 All the royal officials at the king's gate knelt down and paid honor to Haman, for the king had commanded this concerning him. But Mordecai would not kneel down or pay him honor. 3 Then the royal officials at the king's gate asked Mordecai, "Why do you disobey the king's command?" 4 Day after day they spoke to him but he refused to comply. Therefore they told Haman about it to see whether Mordecai's behavior would be tolerated, for he had told them he was a Jew. 5 When Haman saw that Mordecai would not kneel down or pay him honor, he was enraged. 6 Yet having learned who Mordecai's people were, he scorned the idea of killing only Mordecai. Instead Haman looked for a way to destroy all Mordecai's people, the Jews, throughout the whole kingdom of Xerxes. 7 In the twelfth year of King Xerxes, in the first month, the month of Nisan, the pur (that is, the lot) was cast in the presence of Haman to select a day and month. And the lot fell on the twelfth month, the month of Adar. 8 Then Haman said to King Xerxes, "There is a certain people dispersed among the peoples in all the provinces of your kingdom who keep themselves separate. Their customs are different from those of all other people, and they do not obey the king's laws; it is not in the king's best interest to tolerate them. 9 If it pleases the king, let a decree be issued to destroy them, and I will give ten thousand talents of silver to the king's administrators for the royal treasury." 10 So the king took his signet ring from his finger and gave it to Haman son of Hammedatha, the Agagite, the enemy of the

Jews. 11 "Keep the money," the king said to Haman, "and do with the people as you please." 12 Then on the thirteenth day of the first month the royal secretaries were summoned. They wrote out in the script of each province and in the language of each people all Haman's orders to the king's satraps, the governors of the various provinces and the nobles of the various peoples. These were written in the name of King Xerxes himself and sealed with his own ring. 13 Dispatches were sent by couriers to all the king's provinces with the order to destroy, kill and annihilate all the Jews—young and old, women and children—on a single day, the thirteenth day of the twelfth month, the month of Adar, and to plunder their goods. 14 A copy of the text of the edict was to be issued as law in every province and made known to the people of every nationality so they would be ready for that day. 15The couriers went out, spurred on by the king's command, and the edict was issued in the citadel of Susa. The king and Haman sat down to drink, but the city of Susa was bewildered.

Esther 4

When Mordecai learned of all that had been done, he tore his clothes, put on sackcloth and ashes, and went out into the city, wailing loudly and bitterly. But he went only as far as the king's gate, because no one clothed in sackcloth was allowed to enter it. In every province to which the edict and order of the king came, there was great mourning among the Jews, with fasting, weeping and wailing. Many lay in sackcloth and ashes. When Esther's eunuchs and female attendants came and told her about Mordecai, she was in great distress. She sent clothes for him to put on instead of his sackcloth, but he would not accept them. Then Esther summoned Hathak, one of the king's eunuchs assigned to attend her, and ordered him to find out what was troubling Mordecai and why. So

Hathak went out to Mordecai in the open square of the city in front of the king's gate. Mordecai told him everything that had happened to him, including the exact amount of money Haman had promised to pay into the royal treasury for the destruction of the Jews. He also gave him a copy of the text of the edict for their annihilation, which had been published in Susa, to show to Esther and explain it to her, and he told him to instruct her to go into the king's presence to beg for mercy and plead with him for her people. Hathak went back and reported to Esther what Mordecai had said. Then she instructed him to say to Mordecai, "All the king's officials and the people of the royal provinces know that for any man or woman who approaches the king in the inner court without being summoned the king has but one law: that they be put to death unless the king extends the gold scepter to them and spares their lives. But thirty days have passed since I was called to go to the king." When Esther's words were reported to Mordecai, he sent back this answer: "Do not think that because you are in the king's house you alone of all the Jews will escape. For if you remain silent at this time, relief and deliverance for the Jews will arise from another place, but you and your father's family will perish. And who knows but that you have come to your royal position for such a time as this?" Then Esther sent this reply to Mordecai: "Go, gather together all the Jews who are in Susa, and fast for me. Do not eat or drink for three days, night or day. I and my attendants will fast as you do. When this is done, I will go to the king, even though it is against the law. And if I perish, I perish." So Mordecai went away and carried out all of Esther's instructions.

Esther 5

1 On the third day Esther put on her royal robes and stood in the inner court of the palace, in front of the king's hall. The king was sitting on his royal throne in the hall, facing the entrance. When he saw Queen Esther standing in the court, he was pleased with her and held out to her the gold scepter that was in his hand. So Esther approached and touched the tip of the scepter. Then the king asked, "What is it, Queen Esther? What is your request? Even up to half the kingdom, it will be given you." "If it pleases the king," replied Esther, "let the king, together with Haman, come today to a banquet I have prepared for him.""Bring Haman at once," the king said, "so that we may do what Esther asks." So the king and Haman went to the banquet Esther had prepared. As they were drinking wine, the king again asked Esther, "Now what is your petition? It will be given you. And what is your request? Even up to half the kingdom, it will be granted." Esther replied, "My petition and my request is this: If the king regards me with favor and if it pleases the king to grant my petition and fulfill my request, let the king and Haman come tomorrow to the banquet I will prepare for them. Then I will answer the king's question." Haman went out that day happy and in high spirits. But when he saw Mordecai at the king's gate and observed that he neither rose nor showed fear in his presence, he was filled with rage against Mordecai. Nevertheless, Haman restrained himself and went home. Calling together his friends and Zeresh, his wife, Haman boasted to them about his vast wealth, his many sons, and all the ways the king had honored him and how he had elevated him above the other nobles and officials. "And that's not all," Haman added. "I'm the only person Queen Esther invited to accompany the king to the banquet she gave. And she has invited me along with the king tomorrow. But all this gives me no satisfaction as long as I see that Jew Mordecai sitting at the king's gate." His wife Zeresh and all his friends said to him, "Have a pole set up, reaching to a height of fifty cubits, and ask the king in the morning to have Mordecai impaled on it. Then go with the

king to the banquet and enjoy yourself." This suggestion delighted Haman, and he had the pole set up.

Esther 6

1 That night the king could not sleep; so he ordered the book of the chronicles, the record of his reign, to be brought in and read to him. 2 It was found recorded there that Mordecai had exposed Bigthan and Teresh, two of the king's officers who guarded the doorway, who had conspired to assassinate King Xerxes. 3 "What honor and recognition has Mordecai received for this?" the king asked. "Nothing has been done for him," his attendants answered. 4 The king said, "Who is in the court?" Now Haman had just entered the outer court of the palace to speak to the king about impaling Mordecai on the pole he had set up for him. 5 His attendants answered, "Haman is standing in the court." "Bring him in," the king ordered. 6 When Haman entered, the king asked him, "What should be done for the man the king delights to honor?" Now Haman thought to himself, "Who is there that the king would rather honor than me?" 7 So he answered the king, "For the man the king delights to honor, 8 have them bring a royal robe the king has worn and a horse the king has ridden, one with a royal crest placed on its head. 9 Then let the robe and horse be entrusted to one of the king's most noble princes. Let them robe the man the king delights to honor, and lead him on the horse through the city streets, proclaiming before him, 'This is what is done for the man the king delights to honor!' " 10 "Go at once," the king commanded Haman. "Get the robe and the horse and do just as you have suggested for Mordecai the Jew, who sits at the king's gate. Do not neglect anything you have recommended." 11 So Haman got the robe and the horse. He robbed Mordecai, and led him on horseback through the city streets, proclaiming before him, "This is what is done

for the man the king delights to honor!" 12 Afterward Mordecai returned to the king's gate. But Haman rushed home, with his head covered in grief, 13 and told Zeresh his wife and all his friends everything that had happened to him. His advisers and his wife Zeresh said to him, "Since Mordecai, before whom your downfall has started, is of Jewish origin, you cannot stand against him—you will surely come to ruin!" 14 While they were still talking with him, the king's eunuchs arrived and hurried Haman away to the banquet Esther had prepared.

Esther 7

1 So the king and Haman went to Queen Esther's banquet, 2 and as they were drinking wine on the second day, the king again asked, "Queen Esther, what is your petition? It will be given you. What is your request? Even up to half the kingdom, it will be granted." 3 Then Queen Esther answered, "If I have found favor with you, Your Majesty, and if it pleases you, grant me my life—this is my petition. And spare my people—this is my request. 4 For I and my people have been sold to be destroyed, killed and annihilated. If we had merely been sold as male and female slaves, I would have kept quiet, because no such distress would justify disturbing the king. " 5 King Xerxes asked Queen Esther, "Who is he? Where is he—the man who has dared to do such a thing?" 6 Esther said, "An adversary and

enemy! This vile Haman!" And Haman was terrified before the king and queen. 7 The king got up in a rage, left his wine and went out into the palace garden. But Haman, realizing that the king had already decided his fate, stayed behind to beg Queen Esther for his life. 8 Just as the king returned from the palace garden to the banquet hall, Haman was falling on the couch where Esther was reclining. The king exclaimed, "Will he even molest the queen while she is with me in the house?" As soon as the word left the king's mouth, they covered Haman's face. 9 Then Harbona, one of the eunuchs attending the king, said, "A pole reaching to a height of fifty cubits stands by Haman's house. He had it set up for Mordecai, who spoke up to help the king." The king said, "Impale him on it!" 10 So they impaled Haman on the pole he had set up for Mordecai. Then the king's fury subsided.

The story of Queen Esther is important in Rastafari culture because it demonstrates how the Queen used her beauty not to advance herself but her people. Jah wants us to use what we have to do his work. He will do the rest. Blessed.

Rasta Rules

7 Rastafari Rules for Dreadlocks

#1 Dreadlocks are not for sensuality as a Rasta

Dreadlocks must never be used to attract sexual attention. Many people are attracted to people with locks because we have a "different appearance." But to show the dreadlocks intentionally for this purpose is against Rastafari Livity. Dreadlocks as a Rasta, represent a Life that puts King Selassie I at the forefront, and respect for the laws of the Most High Jah. Dreadlocks are not a tool for babylon games of sensuality and sexuality.

#2 Real Rasta Women Cover Locks when in Public!

A Woman of Rastafari livity must have her locks covered in public as to not disrespect herself and her faith. A Rasta women with locks hanging down around her shoulders not covered may be seen as slack, trying to entice sexual attention, or not Rastafari at all. Rasta women cover locks in public so that part of herself is reserved only for her youths, husband, Jah and herself. Every Rasta woman must wear her dreadlocks natural, no chemicals, extensions, hair dyes, locking gels or wax etc.

#3 Every Rasta must have a lock dreadlocks Crown

If you do not have a dreadlocks crown on your head you are not a Rasta. Any Rasta who can grow hair, whose hair is growing, and the hair is not locked he/she has not made the vow and commitment to live as Rastafari.

Part of wearing a dreadlocks crown is to show commitment and fidelity to Jah and to others. This means you are willing to sacrifice the opinions of Babylon, for the faith and knowing of Jah Rastafari Livity as truth and the rightful way of life.

4 Only Family Members can touch the dreadlocks crown

In Rastafari locks are considered holy. The Rasta must decide who he deems fit, closest to him, to touch his holy crown. For some Rasta this means, the spouse only, for others it will mean strictly those of the same blood line. The dreadlocks crown is not to be touched or *ooed and awed* over by strangers, and those who are not Rastafari. This is disrespect to the Most High Jah.

#5 Dreadlocks must be washed at least one time/week

As Rastafari we are very clean. We know Jah only goes where cleanliness is a top priority. Some have a misconception about Rasta...that we do not keep our hair clean. This is so far from the truth. Rasta are some of the cleanest people, but you would have to live with one to know this. Our hair is no exception.

Rasta believe the holy crown is a "spiritual antennae" sending and receiving information from Ancestors and Jah the Creator. What will happen if we allow our antenna to become clogged with build up of dirt? Rasta do not practice such things. For Rasta the dreadlocks must be washed at minimum one time per week. Some Rasta wash locs everyday. Some wash 2x a week if they have been sweating a lot during the week. Once a week is the minimum for every Rastafari.

#6 Dreadlocks are Holy and need to be treated as sacred

Many Rasta Cover dreadlocks as a way of embracing the faith more deeply.

- Keeping dreadlocks clean
- Wearing dreadlock for Jah only (covered in a head wrap)
- Keeping Dreadlocks private (covered in a head wrap)
- Preventing babylon energy from mixing with Rasta energy (covered in a head wrap)

Most Rasta do not allow people we do not know, to touch our hair. Our hair is holy, so only those such as close family members and our selves may touch the dreadlocks. Rasta never goes to a hairdresser, not to start lock, or to maintain them.

#7 Dreadlocks must never be altered in any way
Dreadlocks must never be altered all the days of the life of Rasta this includes

- Cutting
- Dying
- Trimming
- Shaving
- Extensions
- Interlocking
- Lachhooking

Etc.

Dreadlocks as a Rasta must be left to grow natural without chemicals, without heat (blow drying) or any alterations. Give thanks

- [7 Quick Dreadlocks Tips YouTube Video!](#)

The Story of Samson & Delilah

- Is it ok for Rastafari (Nazarite) to do as the heathen do? (prostitution/buying sex, eating from carcass etc.)
- How important is it for a Rasta to keep Jah Commandments?
- After Rasta break Jah commandments what happens is there any consequence?

One day Samson went to Gaza, where he saw a prostitute. He went in to spend the night with her. The people of Gaza were told, "Samson is here!" So they surrounded the place and lay in wait for him all night at the city gate. They made no move during the night, saying, "At dawn we'll kill him."

But Samson lay there only until the middle of the night. Then he got up and took hold of the doors of the city gate, together with the two posts, and tore them loose, bar and all. He lifted them to his shoulders and carried them to the top of the hill that faces Hebron.

Some time later, he fell in love with a woman in the Valley of Sorek whose name was Delilah. The rulers of the Philistines went to her and said, "See if you can lure him into showing you the secret of his great strength and how we can overpower him so we may tie him up and subdue him. Each one of us will give you eleven hundred shekels of silver."

So Delilah said to Samson, "Tell me the secret of your great strength and how you can be tied up and subdued."

Samson answered her, "If anyone ties me with seven fresh bowstrings that have not been dried, I'll become as weak as any other man."

Then the rulers of the Philistines brought her seven fresh bowstrings that had not been dried, and she tied him with them. With men hidden in the room, she called to him, "Samson, the Philistines are upon you!" But he snapped the bowstrings as easily as a piece of string snaps when it comes close to a flame. So the secret of his strength was not discovered.

Then Delilah said to Samson, "You have made a fool of me; you lied to me. Come now, tell me how you can be tied."

He said, "If anyone ties me securely with new ropes that have never been used, I'll become as weak as any other man."

So Delilah took new ropes and tied him with them. Then, with men hidden in the room, she called to him, "Samson, the Philistines are upon you!" But he snapped the ropes off his arms as if they were threads.

Delilah then said to Samson, "All this time you have been making a fool of me and lying to me. Tell me how you can be tied."

He replied, "If you weave the seven braids of my head into the fabric on the loom and tighten it with the pin, I'll become as weak as any other man." So while he was sleeping, Delilah took the seven braids of his head, wove them into the fabric and tightened it with the pin.

Again she called to him, "Samson, the Philistines are upon you!" He awoke from his sleep and pulled up the pin and the loom, with the fabric.

Then she said to him, "How can you say, 'I love you,' when you won't confide in me? This is the third time you have made a fool of me and haven't told me the secret of your great strength." With such nagging she prodded him day after day until he was sick to death of it.

So he told her everything. "No razor has ever been used on my head," he said, "because I have been a Nazirite dedicated to God from my mother's womb. If my head were shaved, my strength would leave me, and I would become as weak as any other man."

When Delilah saw that he had told her everything, she sent word to the rulers of the Philistines, "Come back once more; he has told me everything." So the rulers of the Philistines returned with the silver in their hands. [19] After putting him to sleep on her lap, she called for someone to shave off the seven braids of his hair, and so began to subdue him. And his strength left him.

Then she called, "Samson, the Philistines are upon you!"

He awoke from his sleep and thought, "I'll go out as before and shake myself free." But he did not know that the Lord had left him.

Then the Philistines seized him, gouged out his eyes and took him down to Gaza. Binding him with bronze shackles, they set him to grinding grain in the prison. But the hair on his head began to grow again after it had been shaved.

The Death of Samson

Now the rulers of the Philistines assembled to offer a great sacrifice to Dagon their god and to celebrate, saying, "Our god has delivered Samson, our enemy, into our hands."

When the people saw him, they praised their god, saying,

"Our god has delivered our enemy

    into our hands,

the one who laid waste our land

    and multiplied our slain."

While they were in high spirits, they shouted, "Bring out Samson to entertain us." So they called Samson out of the prison, and he performed for them.

When they stood him among the pillars, Samson said to the servant who held his hand, "Put me where I can feel the pillars that support the temple, so that I may lean against them." Now the temple was crowded with men and women; all the rulers of the Philistines were there, and on the roof were about three thousand men and women watching Samson perform. Then Samson prayed to the Lord,"Sovereign Lord, remember me. Please, God, strengthen me just once more, and let me with one blow get revenge on the Philistines for my two eyes." Then Samson reached toward the two central pillars on which the temple stood. Bracing himself against them, his right hand on the one and his left hand on the other, Samson said, "Let me die with the Philistines!" Then he pushed with all his might, and down came the temple on the rulers and all the people in it. Thus he killed many more when he died than while he lived.

Then his brothers and his father's whole family went down to get him. They brought him back and buried him between Zorah and Eshtaol in the tomb of Manoah his father. He had led Israel twenty years.

4 Rules for dressing as Queens

As Empress being able to carry life is a gift from Jah the creator. Rasta women are Mothers, sisters, wives, and have power over our household, our lives, and naturally we influence those around us. Wearing skirts only helps to separate us as divine feminine from our Masculine counterparts. As Rasta We "fulljoy" long skirts to our ankles, representing the bearers and bringers of life of Jah beautiful design. The skirt may be tight or loose depending our mood and our duties for that particular day.

#1 No off the shoulder shirts or dresses without a covering

Even if the dress is Rasta colored, we must not wear clothing off the shoulder unless the shoulders be covered by another garment such as shall, or a mini jacket. This dress is not suitable with exposed shoulder as a Rasta Empress. This look of exposed shoulders is not part of the uniform of a Rasta woman. Again a simple light jean jacket or shall, and of course head wrap for the locks, would make this dress "Empress appropriate!"

a

#2 Rasta Womens Clothes are her uniform for Jah. Keep it Royal!

When I get up in the morning I look forward to getting dressed and going out to show off my outfit. I want other women to see me and know my clothes are not just clothes, I am wearing a uniform as a woman of Rastafari livity. My clothes represent my mission. My mission is Jah Rastafari. To learn more about the Mission of every Rasta check out my book "How to Become a Rasta." it includes a Rastafari pledge inside, to help one understand fully, what it means to be a Rasta.

#3 Red yellow and green are spiritual colors

Rasta women are encouraged to wear red yellow and green together or even as separate outfits. The yellow will still represent Gold, the Green will still represent nature, the red will still represent the blood shed by babylon.

#4 No exposing or accentuating ass, hips, vagina, or stomach, or breasts as Rasta woman

Rasta women never expose their vagina or stomach or chest in revealing or tight clothing. This means no camel toe tights without a long shirt to cover, no chest pushed up in a bra with breast jiggling for all to watch and, no navel showing, no ass printed in tight jeans, no hips exposed with a long top to cover front only. These examples are sleazy, not Royal. If Empress Menen would not wear it, you should not wear it either, as a new or seasoned Empress. Yes it does matter.

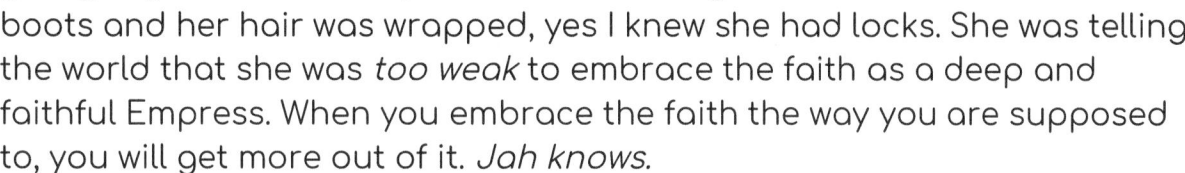

Empress Locks, and exposed ass do not mix!

One day I was downtown in a Rastafari area. I saw this girl, she was wearing tight jeans and a tight top. The jeans imprinted all her ass, and her life giving region in the front, and she had on tight tall boots and her hair was wrapped, yes I knew she had locks. She was telling the world that she was *too weak* to embrace the faith as a deep and faithful Empress. When you embrace the faith the way you are supposed to, you will get more out of it. *Jah knows.*

- *Head covering video!* **On YouTube!!**

4 Bible scriptures on how Empress must dress

1. **A man's garment??** - "A woman shall not wear a man's garment, nor shall a man put on a woman's cloak, for whoever does these things is an abomination to the Lord your God.
2. **Modesty and self control** - Likewise also that women should adorn themselves in respectable apparel, with modesty and self-control, not with braided hair and gold or pearls or costly attire,
3. **Cover hips to the thighs** - You shall make for them linen undergarments to cover their naked flesh. They shall reach from the hips to the thighs;
4. **Imperishable beauty** - Do not let your adorning be external—the braiding of hair and the putting on of gold jewelry, or the clothing you wear— but let your adorning be the hidden person of the heart with the imperishable beauty of a gentle and quiet spirit, which in God's sight is very precious.

For more information about Rasta womens hair, clothing or make, and how to live as an Empress, please read "Life as a Rasta Woman.

- *Journey of a Rasta Woman YouTube Video!*

7 Rasta Rules for the home

#1 No Pharmaceuticals or Medications in the home

Rasta believe there is a natural remedy or cure for everything. That Jah Rastafari provided all that his people needed already in the earth for what concerns us regarding health and nutrition. For this reason many Rasta have at least one natural medicine or natural cures book in the home. Rasta use...

- Herbs/natural remedies
- Vitamins and minerals
- Natural techniques (such as meditation, diet inclusion or elimination, exercise etc)
- Foods (garlic, onion, ginger, ..etc)

For ailments etc. Prescribed medications are taken only when no other option is available. A Rastafari must research all his options before deciding "doctor prescribed" medications will be used in/upon the holy temple of Jah.

Tea Tree oil/Dr. Bronners products
Rasta uses only natural products for cleaning.
I use Tea Tree oil, for cleaning tubs, sinks, toilets and floors. Tea tree oil is a natural essential oil that is a potent cleanser. Mix it with water, or some lime, and natural soap.

#2 A Rastafari home is cleaned Daily
Rasta know Jah does not manifest himself in unclean environments. For this Reason Rasta clean/organize their home daily. We make sure the floor is clean, and all shiny surfaces are wiped down and that there are no lingering stagnant unpleasant odours in any of the rooms.

- Rasta open the windows, in the house, upon waking up to allow fresh air to enter the home.

- We ensure the home is cleaned for the next day using broom and vacuum to clean floors daily, as needed.

- Rasta knows Jah loves a clean home, and that we can feel interact with (create a stronger spiritual channel) him much easier without clutter, dirt, and stagnant air in our surroundings.

#3 No TV Watching as Rasta! No acceptions

Rasta do not watch television! Rasta knows television is just a way for Babylon to brainwash us all to think the same, act the same, and cause us to not think for ourselves. TV also trains us to think that certain people are supposed to think and live a certain way. In other words it causes us to believe stereotypes about other nations/classes/ethnicities/parts of the world etc. Alternatively Rasta...

- Read non fiction books for entertainment
- Watch educational historical documentaries
- Meditate to achieve unity with Jah and the earth
- Write books, poetry, music, and journal to pass the time
- Research about alternative/ natural medicine/healing and medicine to help our children, ourselves, and family members should the need arise

If you do not believe anything written in the book?

If you think any part of this book is *just my opinion.* I encourage you to ask a **born Rastafari**. Ask him/her. How did you get into this faith. If they do not say "I was born that way" do not ask them. If they give the correct response, ask them about any part of this book. All Rasta people know the same things. We are born with it. Watching tv is forbidden as a Rasta.

#4 No meat or meat products in the refrigerator

Not even for others. NO meat, pork, goat, shellfish, oxtail, crab, lobster, chicken, donkey, horse, buffalo. Nothing that can be deemed as carcass should be sitting inside the fridge of a Rastafari.

#5 Most music is "Babylon" music (and lyrics) Only Roots and Culture for Rasta

Most music is Babylon. It's degrading to black people, brainwashing, calling women bitches or something else degrading etc. Rasta play only *Reggae music created by other Rasta,* or love songs (80's is nice, Some of today's love songs are nice too) Music has the ability to affect our thinking and mood, and our lifestyle.

Rasta Reggae Music Artists

- Ras Shiloh
- Junior Kelly
- Dennis Brown
- Sizzla
- Capleton
- Alborosie

Check them out on itunes or YouTube.

5 quick Rasta rules/guidelines for marriage, and socializing

#1 Rasta can marry a christian or another Rasta.

King Selassie I is Christian and Rasta are Israelites.
The person can convert to Rastafari to make the marriage ok. At the same time we don't pay too much attention to the religion of the person as long as they believe in God.

#2 Monogamy is strict in Rastafari Livity.

There is no such thing as Cheating. We Rasta believe if intimacy (sex) with the mate is not enjoyable, then we must stay with our partner regardless. "Bad sex" is not a good enough reason to break up in Rastafari relationships. A Rastafari couples priorities are children, Forward movement in community and family, and serving Jah. Monogamy is the only option.

#3 Rasta can marry any race as long as they believe in God

Rasta embrace other ethnic backgrounds as our brothers and sisters. The important aspect is to live a clean life and Respect the faith of Rastafari, not so much skin color. There are plenty of Rasta who will disagree, and I do understand these aspects. However I am not the owner of anybody else's bed, nor am I the Judge. Jah is in charge of all of that.

#4 Rasta can be friends with anyone.

They can come to our Rastafari home, but we as Rasta must not go to their home to hang out.

#5 Living together constitutes marriage in Rastafari

Marriage is not necessary as a Rastafari couple.

#6 Rasta do not go to bars or clubs unless it is for Rastafari

Clubs and bars usually entertain people who do not practice Rastafari. It is against the livity to go to a bar or club unless it is low key and with a purpose (i.e. business meeting, or to pick up a family member) Plus Rasta do not drink Alcohol so Bar or club is not fit for our faith.

#7 Cheating is not allowed in Sexual Rastafari relationships.

Cheating is an automatic grounds for break up in Rastafari. Cheating sexually is considered an "unclean" act as Rasta. (Read later the 20 Rasta Rules concerning sex) Taken from the bible for the Israelites.

5 guidelines for Raising Rasta children

#1 Rasta children are taught to love & Fear Jah

Rasta children learn very young, that there is a consequence for every action. That there is *one* who sees and knows all things good and bad. His name is Jah, the almighty creator.

#2 Rasta children are taught "Rasta Love"

Rasta children are taught that other nations are their *brothers and sisters*

under Jah. With them we must share, be respectful, and live harmoniously, even if culture or skin color is different. This is how we as Rastafari share "Rasta Love."

#3 Rasta children are taught to be Proud of their Roots & Culture

Rasta Children learn that their heritage is a gift. One of which they should be proud and that Black slavery was an "interruption" in African history, not African history itself, for everyone. All Rasta children regardless of their ethnicity ,learn about African Roots, Culture and History. King Selassie I is an Ethiopian African.

#4 Rasta children are taught to Say "no" to Babylon...

Babylon offers everything. To be a true King or Rasta Queen one must be *speculative.* Rasta teach their

Children that, *not everything is for Royalty,* but that *all is for the heathen.* Rasta children must pause, and think, *before* saying "yes," to anything.

#5 Rasta children are taught to Read the King James Version Bible daily: Rasta couples knows that one can acquire, wisdom, and knowledge, from reading the King James version bible. A Rasta couple encourages their Rasta child to start reading the King James Version bible between age 10-13 on his/her own.

The Story of King Solomon's Wives

King Solomon, however, loved many foreign women besides Pharaoh's daughter—Moabites, Ammonites, Edomites, Sidonians and Hittites. 2 *They were from nations about which the Lord had told the Israelites, "You must not intermarry with them, because they will surely turn your hearts after their gods." Nevertheless, Solomon held fast to them in love.* 3 He had seven hundred wives of royal birth and three hundred concubines, and his wives led him astray. 4 As Solomon grew old, his wives turned his heart after other gods, and his heart was not fully devoted to the Lord his God, as the heart of David his father had been. 5 He followed Ashtoreth the goddess of the Sidonians, and Molek The detestable god of the

Ammonites. **6** So Solomon did evil in the eyes of the Lord; he did not follow the Lord completely, as David his father had done.

On a hill east of Jerusalem, Solomon built a high place for Chemosh the detestable god of Moab, and for Molek the detestable god of the Ammonites. He did the same for all his foreign wives, who burned incense and offered sacrifices to their gods.

The Lord became angry with Solomon because his heart had turned away from the Lord, the God of Israel, who had appeared to him twice.**10** *Although he had forbidden Solomon to follow other gods, Solomon did not keep the Lord's command.* **11** *So the Lord said to Solomon, "Since this is your attitude and you have not kept my covenant and my decrees, which I commanded you, I will most certainly tear the kingdom away from you and give it to one of your subordinates.* **12** Nevertheless, for the sake of David your father, I will not do it during your lifetime. I will tear it out of the hand of your son. **13** Yet I will not tear the whole kingdom from him, but will give him one tribe for the sake of David my servant and for the sake of Jerusalem, which I have chosen."

Rasta Rules

6 Rasta rules/guidelines for Ital Food cooking

Rastafari eat "No Meat":

As Rasta we do not eat or cook beef, pork, shell-fish, or anything that has a hoof and chews a cud, as written in the bible. Rastas are primarily vegan. We eat a lot of Salad, soup and fresh fruits and vegetables.

Rastas choose to cook without Salt:

This is what makes the food Ital. Natural and clean. If Rasta must use salt <u>we use sea salt only.</u>

- <u>Sea salt</u>
- <u>Mountain salt</u>
- <u>Some seasonings</u>

Rasta aim for Abundance of Flavor in Italian Cooking:

When Rasta cook we aim to make the food flavorful *without the use of salt*. We use allspice, or we use onion garlic, thyme and tomato

pimento, scallion, black pepper, coconut for flavor.

7 Common Spices used in Rasta cooking

1. Turmeric
2. Curry powder
3. Onion powder
4. Garlic powder
5. Ginger
6. Coriander
7. All spice

Rasta eats only Fish with Scales:

"These ye shall eat of all that are in the waters: all that have fins and scales shall ye eat: And whatsoever hath not fins and scales ye may not eat; it is unclean unto you."

Many Rasta love to eat fish, and some Rasta are Vegan. It is a rule from the bible for our spirituality (the Nazarite vow) (Deuteronomy and numbers) that we only eat fish with scales. Salt fish, red herring, king fish, are some Rastafari favorites. *Rasta does not eat shell-fish, such as shrimp, or lobster, or crab, as they clean the bottom of the sea, and do not have scales and fins, and are therefore unclean for Rasta to eat.*

Rasta cooking often includes Protein and greens:

Rasta knows it is important to eat a diet that promotes strength, especially when one is vegetarian or vegan. Rasta love to incorporate forms of protein and greens and other strength building foods in with their cooking such as beans, peas, nuts and greens, such as callaloo, okra, Yam, green bana

Rasta food Color and texture:

There is an old saying "People eat with their eyes" You may mix some yellow ackee, with some green calaloo. Or dash some orange pumpkin in with white rice, Jah likes when we include various colored and textured food because it allows us enjoy the food exactly the way the earth grows the food for us.

- Squash
- Yams
- Okra
- Cabbage
- Carrots
- Ackee
- Peas
- Red kidney beans
- Brown lentils
- Yellow corn
- Green spinach

[Try this recipe for INdian Style veggie Chunks](#) Recipe!

Why it's not ok for Rasta to eat meat!

"'Every creature that moves along the ground is to be regarded as unclean; it is not to be eaten. You are not to eat any creature that moves along the ground, whether it moves on its belly or walks on all fours or on many feet; it is unclean. Do not defile yourselves by any of these creatures. Do not make yourselves unclean by means of them or be made unclean by them. I am the Lord your Jah; consecrate yourselves and be holy, because I am holy. **Do not make yourselves unclean by any creature that moves along the ground.** I am the Lord, who brought you up out of Egypt to be your Jah; therefore be holy, because I am holy.

"'These are the regulations concerning animals, birds, every living thing that moves about in the water and every creature that moves along the ground. You must distinguish between the unclean and the clean, between living creatures that may be eaten and those that may not be eaten.'"

20 Rasta Rules & Laws about sex

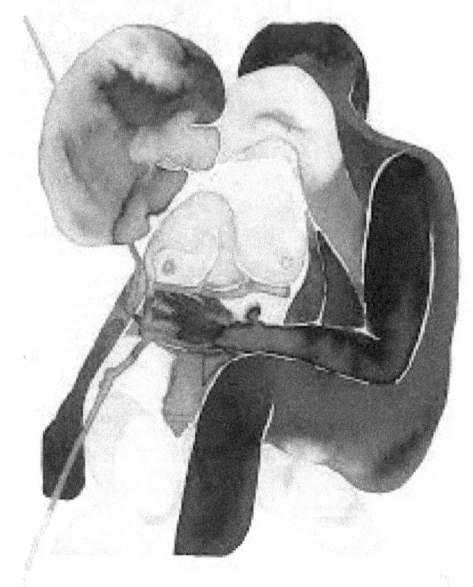

You may find some of these rule to be obvious. But what's obvious to you may not be obvious to others. I did not write these rules laws and commands, they can be found in the King James Version Bible.

1. "'No one is to approach any close relative to have sexual relations. I am the Lord.
2. "'Do not dishonor your father by having sexual relations with your mother. She is your mother; do not have relations with her.
3. "'Do not have sexual relations with your father's wife; that would dishonor your father.

4. "'Do not have sexual relations with your sister, either your father's daughter or your mother's daughter, whether she was born in the same home or elsewhere.
5. "Do not have sexual relations with your son's daughter or your daughter's daughter; that would dishonor you.
6. "Do not have sexual relations with the daughter of your father's wife, born to your father; she is your sister.
7. "'Do not have sexual relations with your father's sister; she is your father's close relative.
8. "'Do not have sexual relations with your mother's sister, because she is your mother's close relative.
9. "'Do not dishonor your father's brother by approaching his wife to have sexual relations; she is your aunt.
10. "'Do not have sexual relations with your daughter-in-law. She is your son's wife; do not have relations with her.
11. "'Do not have sexual relations with your brother's wife; that would dishonor your brother.
12. "'Do not have sexual relations with both a woman and her daughter. Do not have sexual relations with either her son's daughter or her daughter's daughter; they are her close relatives. That is wickedness.
13. "'Do not take your wife's sister as a rival wife and have sexual relations with her while your wife is living.
14. "'Do not approach a woman to have sexual relations during the uncleanness of her monthly period.
15. "'Do not have sexual relations with your neighbor's wife and defile yourself with her.
16. "'Do not give any of your children to be sacrificed to Molek, for you must not profane the name of your Jah. I am the Lord.

17. "'Do not have sexual relations with a man as one does with a woman; that is detestable.
18. "'Do not have sexual relations with an animal and defile yourself with it. A woman must not present herself to an animal to have sexual relations with it; that is a perversion.
19. "'Do not defile yourselves in any of these ways, because this is how the nations that I am going to drive out before you became defiled. Even the land was defiled; so I punished it for its sin, and the land vomited out its inhabitants. But you must keep my decrees and my laws. The native-born and the foreigners residing among you must not do any of these detestable things, for all these things were done by the people who lived in the land before you, and the land became defiled. And if you defile the land, it will vomit you out as it vomited out the nations that were before you.
20. "'Everyone who does any of these detestable things—such persons must be cut off from their people. Keep my requirements and do not follow any of the detestable customs that were practiced before you came and do not defile yourselves with them. I am the Lord your God.'"

20 Various Laws for Rasta

The Lord said to Moses, "Speak to the entire assembly of Israel and say to them: 'Be holy because I, the Lord your Jah, am holy.

"Each of you must respect your mother and father, and you must observe my Sabbaths. I am the Lord your Jah.

"'Do not turn to idols or make metal Jahs for yourselves. I am the Lord your Jah.

"'When you sacrifice a fellowship offering to the Lord, sacrifice it in such a way that it will be accepted on your behalf. It shall be eaten on the day you sacrifice it or on the next day; anything left over until the third day must be burned up. If any of it is eaten on the third day, it is impure and will not

67

be accepted. Whoever eats it will be held responsible because they have desecrated what is holy to the Lord; they must be cut off from their people.

"When you reap the harvest of your land, do not reap to the very edges of your field or gather the gleanings of your harvest. Do not go over your vineyard a second time or pick up the grapes that have fallen. Leave them for the poor and the foreigner. I am the Lord your Jah.

"Do not steal.

"Do not lie.

"Do not deceive one another.

"Do not swear falsely by my name and so profane the name of your Jah. I am the Lord.

"Do not defraud or rob your neighbor.

"Do not hold back the wages of a hired worker overnight.

"Do not curse the deaf or put a stumbling block in front of the blind, but fear your Jah. I am the Lord.

"'Do not pervert justice; do not show partiality to the poor or favoritism to the great, but judge your neighbor fairly.

"'Do not go about spreading slander among your people.

"'Do not do anything that endangers your neighbor's life. I am the Lord.

"'Do not hate a fellow Israelite in your heart. Rebuke your neighbor frankly so you will not share in their guilt.

"'Do not seek revenge or bear a grudge against anyone among your people, but love your neighbor as yourself. I am the Lord.

"'Keep my decrees.

"'Do not mate different kinds of animals.

"'Do not plant your field with two kinds of seed.

"'Do not wear clothing woven of two kinds of material.

"'If a man sleeps with a female slave who is promised to another man but who has not been ransomed or given her freedom, there must be due punishment. Yet they are not to be put to death, because she had not been freed. The man, however, must bring a ram to the entrance to the tent of meeting for a guilt offering to the Lord. With the ram of the guilt offering the priest is to make atonement for him before the Lord for the sin he has committed, and his sin will be forgiven.

"'When you enter the land and plant any kind of fruit tree, regard its fruit as forbidden. For three years you are to consider it forbidden[c]; it must not be eaten. In the fourth year all its fruit will be holy, an offering of praise to the Lord. But in the fifth year you may eat its fruit. In this way your harvest will be increased. I am the Lord your Jah.

"'Do not eat any meat with the blood still in it.

"'Do not practice divination or seek omens.

"'Do not cut the hair at the sides of your head or clip off the edges of your beard.

"'Do not cut your bodies for the dead or put tattoo marks on yourselves. I am the Lord.

"'Do not degrade your daughter by making her a prostitute, or the land will turn to prostitution and be filled with wickedness.

"'Observe my Sabbaths and have reverence for my sanctuary. I am the Lord.

"'Do not turn to mediums or seek out spiritists, for you will be defiled by them. I am the Lord your Jah.

"'Stand up in the presence of the aged, show respect for the elderly and revere your Jah. I am the Lord.

"'When a foreigner resides among you in your land, do not mistreat them. 34 The foreigner residing among you must be treated as your native-born. Love them as yourself, for you were foreigners in Egypt. I am the Lord your Jah.

"'Do not use dishonest standards when measuring length, weight or quantity. **36** Use honest scales and honest weights, an honest ephah and an honest hin. I am the Lord your Jah, who brought you out of Egypt.

"'Keep all my decrees and all my laws and follow them. I am the Lord.'"

6 Blessings of Obedience to Jah Rastafari

Do not make idols or set up an image or a sacred stone for yourselves, and do not place a carved stone in your land to bow down before it. I am the Lord your Jah.

Observe my Sabbaths and have reverence for my sanctuary. I am the Lord.

If you follow my decrees and are careful to obey my commands...

1. **Jah provides Prosperity -** *"...I will send you rain in its season, and the ground will yield its crops and the trees their fruit..."*

2. **Jah provides Full Stomach and Protection -** *"...Your threshing will continue until grape harvest and the grape harvest will continue until planting, and you will eat all the food you want and live in safety in your land..."*
3. **Jah provides Peace -** *"...I will grant peace in the land, and you will lie down and no one will make you afraid. I will remove wild beasts from the land, and the sword will not pass through your country..."*
4. **Jah provides Strength and Fortitude as a Rasta -** You will pursue your enemies, and they will fall by the sword before you. Five of you will chase a hundred, and a hundred of you will chase ten thousand, and your enemies will fall by the sword before you.

5. **Jah will keep all his promises to Dedicated Rasta** - I will look on you with favor and make you fruitful and increase your numbers, and I will keep my covenant with you.
6. **Jah provides Abundance and Love** - You will still be eating last year's harvest when you will have to move it out to make room for the new. I will put my dwelling place among you, and I will not abhor you.

I will walk among you and be your God, and you will be my people. I am the Lord your God, who brought you out of Egypt so that you would no longer be slaves to the Egyptians; I broke the bars of your yoke and enabled you to walk with heads held high.

5 Punishments for breaking Jah Rastafari Rules

...But if you will not listen to me and carry out all these commands,15 and if you reject my decrees and abhor my laws and fail to carry out all my commands and so violate my covenant, then I will do this to you:

#1 Punishment for breaking Jah Rules

I will bring on you sudden terror, wasting diseases and fever that will destroy your sight and sap your strength. You will plant seed in vain, because your enemies will eat it.

#2 Punishment for breaking Jah Rules

I will set my face against you so that you will be defeated by your enemies; those who hate you will rule over you, and you will flee even when no one is pursuing you.

#3 Punishment for breaking Jah Rules

If after all this you will not listen to me, I will punish you for your sins seven times over. I will break down your stubborn pride and make the sky above you like iron and the ground beneath you like bronze. Your strength will be spent in vain, because your soil will not yield its crops, nor will the trees of your land yield their fruit.

#4 Punishment for breaking Jah Rules

If you remain hostile toward me and refuse to listen to me, I will multiply your afflictions seven times over, as your sins deserve. I will send wild animals against you, and they will rob you of your children, destroy your cattle and make you so few in number that your roads will be deserted.

#5 Punishment for breaking Jah Rules

If in spite of these things you do not accept my correction but continue to be hostile toward me, I myself will be hostile toward you and will afflict you for your sins seven times over. And I will bring the sword on you to avenge the breaking of the covenant. When you withdraw into your cities, I will send a plague among you, and you will be given into enemy hands. When I cut off your supply of bread, ten women will be able to bake your bread in one oven, and they will dole out the bread by weight. You will eat, but you will not be satisfied. If in spite of this you still do not listen to me but continue to be hostile toward me, then in my anger I will be hostile toward you, and I myself will punish you for your sins seven times over. You will eat the flesh of your sons and the flesh of your daughters. I will destroy your high places, cut down your incense altars and pile your dead bodies on the lifeless forms of your idols, and I will abhor you. I will turn your cities into ruins and lay waste your sanctuaries, and I will take no delight in the pleasing aroma of your offerings. I myself will lay waste the land, so that your enemies who live there will be appalled. I will scatter you among the nations and will draw out my sword and pursue you. Your land will be laid waste, and your cities will lie in ruins. Then the land will enjoy its sabbath years all the time that it lies desolate and you are in the country of your enemies; then the land will rest and enjoy its sabbaths. All the time that it lies desolate, the land will have the rest it did not have during the sabbaths you lived in it. As for those of you who are left, I will make their hearts so fearful in the lands of their enemies that the sound of a windblown leaf will put them to flight. They will run as though fleeing from the sword, and they will fall, even though no one is pursuing them. They will stumble over one another as though fleeing from the sword, even though no one is pursuing them. So you will not be able to stand before your enemies. You will perish among the nations; the land of your enemies will devour you. Those of you who are left will waste away in the lands of their enemies because of their sins; also because of their ancestors' sins they will waste away.

Rasta Confession....

But if they will confess their sins and the sins of their ancestors—their unfaithfulness and their hostility toward me, which made me hostile toward them so that I sent them into the land of their enemies—then when their uncircumcised hearts are humbled and they pay for their sin, I will remember my covenant with Jacob and my covenant with Isaac and my covenant with Abraham, and I will remember the land. For the land will be deserted by them and will enjoy its sabbaths while it lies desolate without them. They will pay for their sins because they rejected my laws and abhorred my decrees. Yet in spite of this, when they are in the land of their enemies, I will not reject them or abhor them so as to destroy them completely, breaking my covenant with them. I am the Lord their Jah. **45** But for their sake I will remember the covenant with their ancestors whom I brought out of Egypt in the sight of the nations to be their Jah. I am the Lord.'"

These are the decrees, the laws and the regulations that the Lord established at Mount Sinai between himself and the Israelites through Moses.

If you want to be a Rasta, be a Rasta for life, or don't do it at all.

9 Rules of The Jah Rastafari Holy Sabbath

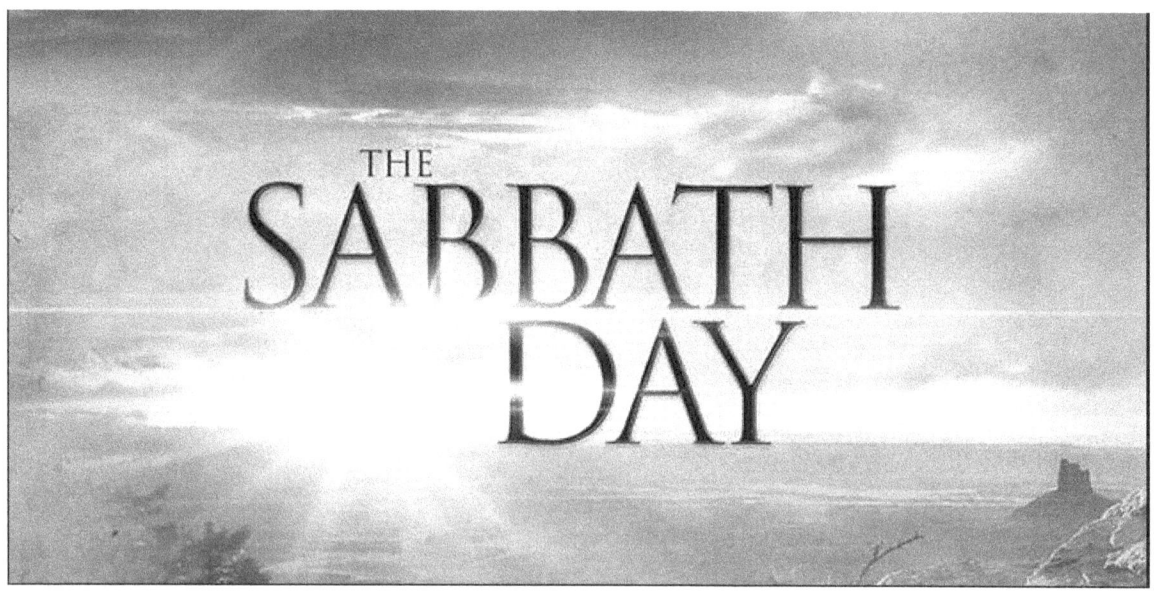

When is the Rastafari holy Sabbath day?

The sabbath day is every Saturday of every month without exception. The Sabbath starts every Friday at about 5:30 pm and continues until Saturday at 5:30pm. The following is a list of rules for Keeping Jah Rastafari Holy Sabbath Day, and keeping it holy.

9 Things Rasta must not do....during the holy Sabbath

1. Work on the holy Sabbath
2. Go to clubs or to bar
3. Go to friends house
4. Have friends over during Sabbath
5. Watch Television
6. Curse and swear
7. Eat solid food
8. Sex

9. Work out or go to the Gym

The reason the rules for the Sabbath day are so strict is because This is a time for Jah *to feel our rest*. Jah blesses us as Rasta when he *can feel our Rest*. By dedicating yourself to him and/on the Sabbath we have made *living sacrifices in honor of the High one*. Practice the Sabbath correct and reap the rewards of Jah Rastafari.

6 things Rasta are encouraged to do....during the Sabbath

1. Meditate/pray
2. Clean the home
3. Prepare nice Ital food for the feast (end of the Sabbath)
4. Drink natural fruit Juice or tea

5. Read and study his bible
6. Listen to Rastafari Reggae music
7. Organize the home or work tools
8. Write spiritual poetry or music, or song lyrics.
9. Sit in silence for 20 mins at a time as a way of dedicating oneself to Jah

Honor to Jah on the Sabbath Day!

These encouraged activities during the Sabbath Day of Rastafari, Raise our vibration as Rasta and do not violate the holy Sabbath Day. Drinking only natural fruit juices and abstaining from solid foods, allows for the holy temple of Rasta, to be dedicated to Jah during the Sabbath. Jah loves when we honor him, especially on the Sabbath day. Blessings upon blessings, upon blessings.

10 Rasta Rules every Rasta knows

1. I am the Lord your Jah, You shall have no other Jah before me.
2. You shall not use the Lord's Name in vain.
3. Remember to keep Sabbath day holy.
4. Honour your father and mother.
5. You shall not commit murder.
6. You shall not commit adultery.
7. You shall not steal.
8. You shall not bear false witness against your neighbor.
9. You shall not covet your neighbor's wife.
10. You shall not covet your neighbor's goods.

3 Rasta Rules for Holiness and purity

"And the LORD spake unto Moses, saying, Speak unto the children of Israel, and say unto them, When either man or woman shall separate themselves to vow a vow of a Nazarite, to separate themselves unto the LORD

#1 Rasta must Avoid Strong Drink

He shall separate himself from wine and strong drink, and shall

drink no vinegar of wine, or vinegar of strong drink, neither shall he drink any liquor of grapes, nor eat moist grapes, or dried. All the days of his separation shall he eat nothing that is made of the vine tree, from the kernels even to the husk.

#2 No Razor upon the head of a Rasta

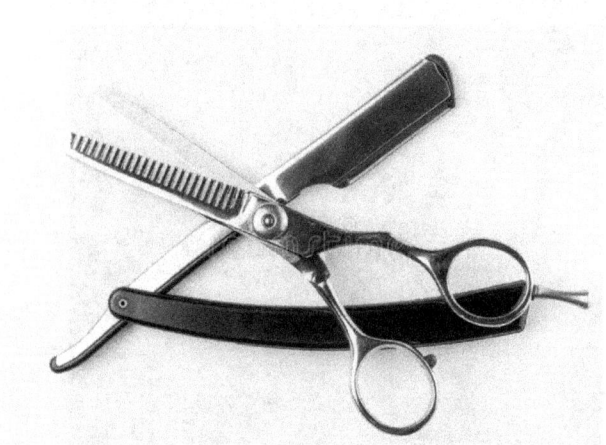

All the days of the vow of his separation there shall no razor come upon his head: until the days be fulfilled, in the which he separated himself unto the LORD, he shall be holy, and shall let the locks of the hair of his head grow.

#3 Rasta must stay away from all carcass

All the days that he separated himself unto the LORD he shall come at no dead body. He shall not make himself unclean for his father, or for his mother, for his brother, or for his sister, when they die: because the consecration of his Jah is upon his head. All the days of his separation

he is holy unto the LORD.

And if any man died very suddenly by him, and he hath defiled the head of his consecration; then he shall shave his head in the day of his cleansing, on the seventh day shall he shave it. And on the eighth day he shall bring two turtles, or two young pigeons, to the priest, to the door of the tabernacle of the congregation: And the priest shall offer the one for a sin offering, and the other for a burnt offering, and make an atonement for him, for that he sinned by the dead, and shall hallow his head that same day. And he shall consecrate unto the LORD the days of his separation, and shall bring a lamb of the first year for a trespass offering: but the days that were before shall be lost, because his separation was defiled..."

This is the law of the Nazarite who hath vowed, and of his offering unto the LORD for his separation, beside that that his hand shall get: according to the vow which he vowed, so he must do after the law of his separation.

5 King Selassie I Rules in Quotes

Haile Selassie I Quote/Rule #1: sharing with the poor

"...a way of life in which the blessings and benefits of the modern world can be enjoyed by all."

Haile Selassie I Quote/Rule #2: Equality ".

..above all, Ethiopia is dedicated to the principle of the equality of all men, irrespective of differences of race, color or creed."

Haile Selassie I Quote/Rule#3: Discrimination

"...as we do not practice or permit discrimination within our nation, so we oppose it wherever it is found."

Haile Selassie I Quote/Rule #4: Religion

"...as we guarantee to each the right to worship as he chooses, so we denounce the policy which sets man against man on issues of religion."

Haile Selassie I Quote/Rule #5: Racism

"...as we extend the hand of universal brotherhood to all, without regard to race or color, so we condemn any social or political order which distinguishes among God's children on this most specious of grounds."

5 Important Rastafari Holidays

Most Rastafari holidays are about celebrating our beloved King His Imperial Majesty, Emperor Haile Selassie. Rasta celebrate, the day he arrived in Jamaica, his birthday, and ofcourse the date King Selassie I and Empress Menen were crowned King and Queen of Ethiopia. You can celebrate them too by cooking a special Ital meal, playing some nice Rasta Reggae Musica and hanging some Photos of his Majesty and Her Majesty in the home. Be sure to have some speeches lined up to read out by or for the children too.

The Nyahbinghi Order in Jamaica celebrates for 7 days and nights the following events:

- **7 January** - Ethiopian Nativity of Christ
- **21 April** - Visit of H.I.M. to Jamaica 1966
- **25 May** - All African Liberation Day
- **23 July** -Birth of HAILE SELASSIE I 1892
- **11 September** - Ethiopian New Year
- **2 November** - H.I.M. Coronation 1930

The more general rule concerning holidays is that Rasta do not celebrate holidays created and embraced by babylon. Please read the real story of how Thanksgiving Holiday got started. Then you will understand….We must do our research before we celebrate any holiday people. The following holidays are not celebrated by Rastafari.

- Christmas
- Easter
- Thanksgiving

Thank you for fulljoying this book. Please share your thoughts about it on amazon.com.

One Love.

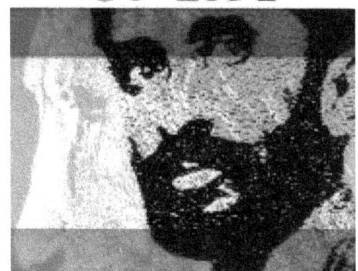

Rasta Way of Life

Life as a Rasta Woman

Ital Rasta eCookbook

Convert to Rastafari

www.jamaicanrastafarianlove.com
www.jamaicanloveblog.wordpress.com

CPSIA information can be obtained
at www.ICGtesting.com
Printed in the USA
LVHW051734070721
692086LV00007B/372